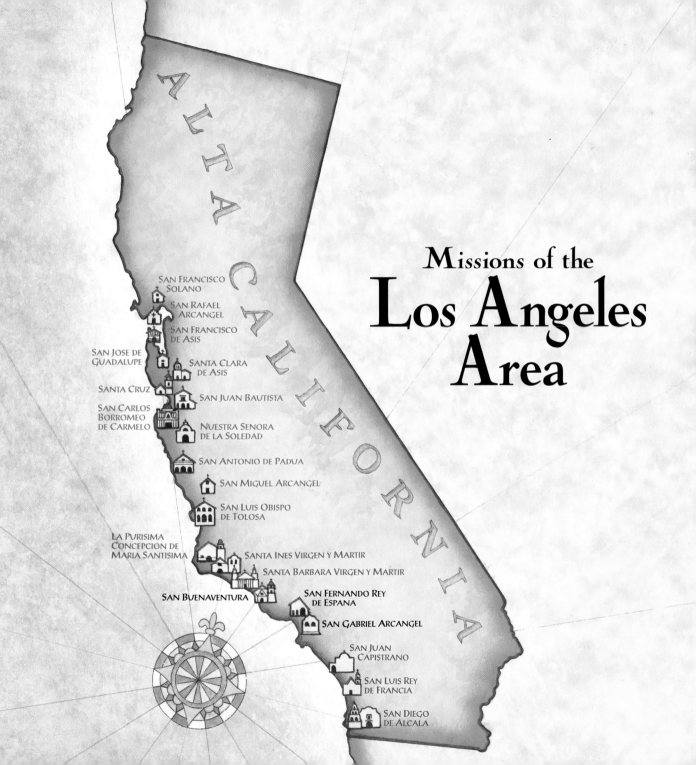

Missions of the
Los Angeles
Area

ALTA CALIFORNIA

San Francisco Solano
San Rafael Arcangel
San Francisco de Asis
San Jose de Guadalupe
Santa Clara de Asis
Santa Cruz
San Juan Bautista
San Carlos Borromeo de Carmelo
Nuestra Senora de la Soledad
San Antonio de Padua
San Miguel Arcangel
San Luis Obispo de Tolosa
La Purisima Concepcion de Maria Santisima
Santa Ines Virgen y Martir
Santa Barbara Virgen y Martir
San Buenaventura
San Fernando Rey de Espana
San Gabriel Arcangel
San Juan Capistrano
San Luis Rey de Francia
San Diego de Alcala

California
MISSIONS

Missions of the
Los Angeles
Area

Dianne MacMillan

LERNER PUBLICATIONS COMPANY

Series editors: Elizabeth Verdick, Mary M. Rodgers, Karen Chernyaev
Series photo researcher: Amy Cox
Series designer: Zachary Marell

Every effort has been made to secure permission for the quoted material and for the photographs in this book.

LIBRARY OF CONGRESS CATALOGING-IN-PUBLICATION DATA

MacMillan, Dianne.
    Missions of the Los Angeles Area / by Dianne MacMillan.
        p. cm.—(California Missions)
    Includes index.
    Summary: Charts the histories of the missions of San Gabriel Arcángel, San Buenaventura, and San Fernando Rey de España, and briefly describes life among the Tongva (Gabrielino) and Chumash Indians before the arrival of the Spaniards.
    ISBN 0–8225–1927–5 (lib. bdg.)
    1. Spanish mission buildings—California—Los Angeles Region—Juvenile literature.
    2. Los Angeles Region (Calif.)—History—Juvenile literature. [1. Missions—California.
    2. California—History. 3. Chumash Indians—Missions—California. 4. Gabrielino Indians—Missions—California. 5. Indians of North America—Missions—California.]
    I. Title II. Series.
    F869.L88A24 1996
    979.4'6—dc20   95–16717
                                                                          CIP
                                                                           AC

Manufactured in the United States of America
1 2 3 4 5 6 – JR – 01 00 99 98 97 96

Cover: *This passageway covered with flowers and vines welcomes visitors to the mission of San Gabriel Arcángel, founded in 1771.* Title page: *Long corridors, such as this one at San Fernando Rey de España, are familiar sights at the California missions.*

CONTENTS

GLOSSARY

adobe: A type of clay soil found in Mexico and in dry parts of the United States. In Alta California, workers formed wet adobe into bricks that hardened in the sun.

Alta California (Upper California): An old Spanish name for the present-day state of California.

Baja California (Lower California): A strip of land off the northwestern coast of Mexico that lies between the Pacific Ocean and the Gulf of California. Part of Mexico, Baja California borders the U.S. state of California.

Franciscan: A member of the Order of Friars Minor, a Roman Catholic community founded in Italy by Saint Francis of Assisi in 1209. The Franciscans are dedicated to performing missionary work and acts of charity.

mission: A center where missionaries (religious teachers) work to spread their beliefs to other people and to teach a new way of life.

missionary: A person sent out by a religious group to spread its beliefs to other people.

neophyte: A Greek word meaning "newly converted" that refers to an Indian baptized into the Roman Catholic community.

New Spain: A large area once belonging to Spain that included what are now the southwestern United States and Mexico. After 1821, when New Spain had gained its independence from the Spanish Empire, the region became known as the Republic of Mexico.

presidio: A Spanish fort for housing soldiers. In Alta California, Spaniards built presidios to protect the missions and priests from possible attacks and to enforce order in the region. California's four main presidios were located at San Diego, Santa Barbara, Monterey, and San Francisco.

quadrangle: A four-sided enclosure surrounded by buildings.

reservation: Tracts of land set aside by the U.S. government to be used by Native Americans.

secularization: A series of laws enacted by the Mexican government in the 1830s. The rulings aimed to take mission land and buildings from Franciscan control and to place the churches in the hands of parish priests, who didn't perform missionary work. Much of the land was distributed to families and individuals.

PRONUNCIATION GUIDE*

Chumash	CHOO-mash
El Camino Reál	el kah-MEE-no ray-AHL
Fernandeños	fair-nahn-DAY-nyohs
Figueroa, José	fee-gay-ROH-ah, hoh-SAY
Gabrielinos	gah-bree-ehl-EEN-ohs
Lasuén, Fermín de	lah-soo-AYN, fair-MEEN day
San Buenaventura	SAHN BWAY-nah-ven-too-rah
San Fernando Rey de España	SAHN fair-NAHN-doh RAY day es-PAH-nyah
San Gabriel Arcángel	SAHN gah-bree-EHL ar-KAHN-hel
Señán, José	say-NYAN, hoh-SAY
Serra, Junípero	SEH-rrah, hoo-NEE-pay-roh
Tongva	TAHNG-vuh
Toypurina	TOY-puh-ree-nuh
Zalvidea, José María	sahl-vee-DAY-ah, hoh-SAY mah-REE-ah

* Local pronunciations may differ.

PREFACE

The religious beliefs and traditions of the Indians of California teach that the blessings of a rich land and a mild climate are gifts from the Creator. The Indians show their love and respect for the Creator—and for all of creation—by carefully managing the land for future generations and by living in harmony with the natural environment.

Over the course of many centuries, the Indians of California organized small, independent societies. Only in the hot, dry deserts of southeastern California did they farm the land to feed themselves. Elsewhere, the abundance of fish, deer, antelope, waterfowl, and wild seeds supplied all that the Indians needed for survival. The economies of these societies did not create huge surpluses of food. Instead the people produced only what they expected would meet their needs. Yet there is no record of famine during the long period when Indians in California managed the land.

These age-old beliefs and practices stood in sharp contrast to the policies of the Spaniards who began to settle areas of California in the late 1700s. Spain established religious missions along the coast to anchor its empire in California. At these missions, Spanish priests baptized thousands of Indians into the Roman Catholic religion. Instead of continuing to hunt and gather their food, the Indians were made to work on mission estates where farming supported the settlements. Pastures for mission livestock soon took over Indian land, and European farming activities depleted native plants. Illnesses that the Spaniards had unintentionally carried from Europe brought additional suffering to many Indian groups.

The Indians living in California numbered 340,000 in the late 1700s, but only 100,000 remained after roughly 70 years of Spanish missionization. Many of the Indians died from disease. Spanish soldiers killed other Indians during native revolts at the missions. Some entire Indian societies were wiped out.

Thousands of mission Indian descendants proudly continue to practice their native culture and to speak their native language. But what is most important to these survivors is that their people's history be understood by those who now call California home, as well as by others across the nation. Through this series of books, young readers will learn for the first time how the missions affected the Indians and their traditional societies.

Perhaps one of the key lessons to be learned from an honest and evenhanded account of California's missions is that the Indians had something important to teach the Spaniards and the people who came to the region later. Our ancestors and today's elders instill in us that we must respect and live in harmony with animals, plants, and one another. While this is an ancient wisdom, it seems especially relevant to our future survival.

Professor Edward D. Castillo
Cahuilla-Luiseño Mission Indian Descendant

INTRODUCTION

FOUNDED BY SPAIN, THE CALIFORNIA **MISSIONS** ARE located on a narrow strip of California's Pacific coast. Some of the historic buildings sit near present-day Highway 101, which roughly follows what was once a roadway called El Camino Reál (the Royal Road), so named to honor the king of Spain. The trail linked a chain of 21 missions set up between 1769 and 1823.

Spain, along with leaders of the Roman Catholic Church, established missions and *presidios* (forts) throughout the Spanish Empire to strengthen its claim to the land. In the 1600s, Spain built mission settlements on the peninsula known as **Baja California,** as well as in other areas of **New Spain** (present-day Mexico).

The goal of the Spanish mission system in North America was to make Indians accept Spanish ways and become loyal subjects of the Spanish king. Priests functioning as **missionaries** (religious teachers) tried to convert the local Indian populations to Catholicism and to

In the mid-1700s, Native Americans living in what is now California came into contact with Roman Catholic missionaries from Spain.

11

teach them to dress and behave like Spaniards. Soldiers came to protect the missionaries and to make sure the Indians obeyed the priests.

During the late 1700s, Spain wanted to spread its authority northward from Baja California into the region known as **Alta California,** where Spain's settlement pattern would be repeated. The first group of Spanish soldiers and missionaries traveled to Alta California in 1769. The missionaries, priests of the **Franciscan** order, were led by Junípero Serra, the father-president of the mission system.

The soldiers and missionaries came into contact with communities of Native Americans, or Indians, that dotted the coastal and inland areas of Alta California. For thousands of years, the region had been home to many Native American groups that spoke a wide variety of languages. Using these Indians as unpaid laborers was vital to the success of the mission system. The mission economy was based on agriculture—a way of life unfamiliar to local Indians, who mostly hunted game and gathered wild plants for food.

Although some Indians willingly joined the missions, the Franciscans relied on various methods to convince or force other Native Americans to become part of the mission system. The priests sometimes lured Indians with gifts of glass beads and colored cloth or other items new to the Native Americans. Some Indians who lost their hunting and food-gathering grounds to mission farms and ranches joined the Spanish settlements to survive. In other cases, Spanish soldiers forcibly took villagers from their homes.

Neophytes, or Indians recruited into the missions, were expected to learn the Catholic faith and the skills for farming and building. Afterward—Spain reasoned—the Native Americans would be able to manage the property themselves, a process that officials figured would take 10 years. But a much different turn of events took place.

Father Junípero Serra, a priest of the Franciscan religious order, dreamed of setting up missions in Alta California (modern-day California) and of teaching the Roman Catholic faith to the local Indians. He founded the first mission, San Diego de Alcalá, in 1769 and went on to establish eight more missions before his death in 1784.

Under the direction of Franciscan priests, the Native Americans at the missions constructed buildings, planted crops, and tended livestock.

Forced to abandon their villages and to give up their age-old traditions, many Native Americans didn't adjust to mission life. In fact, most Indians died soon after entering the missions—mainly from European diseases that eventually killed thousands of Indians throughout California.

Because hundreds of Indian laborers worked at each mission, most of the settlements thrived. The missions produced grapes, olives, wheat, cattle hides, cloth, soap, candles, and other goods. In fact, the missions successfully introduced to Alta California a variety of crops and livestock that still benefit present-day Californians.

The missions became so productive that the Franciscans established a valuable trade network. Mission priests exchanged goods and provided nearby soldiers and settlers with provisions. The agricultural wealth of the missions angered many settlers and soldiers, who resented the priests for holding Alta California's most fertile land and the majority of the livestock and for controlling the Indian labor force.

This resentment grew stronger after 1821, when New Spain became the independent country of Mexico. Mexico claimed Alta California and began the **secularization** of the missions. The mission churches still offered religious services, but the Spanish Franciscans were to be replaced by secular priests. These priests weren't missionaries seeking to convert people.

By 1836 the neophytes were free to leave the missions, and the settlements quickly declined from the loss of workers. Few of the former neophytes found success away from the missions, however. Many continued as forced laborers on the *ranchos* (ranches) or in nearby *pueblos* (towns), earning little or no pay.

In 1848 Mexico lost a war against the United States and ceded Alta California to the U.S. government. By that time, about half of Alta California's Indian population had died. Neophytes who had remained at the missions often had no village to which to return. They moved

CALIFORNIA MISSION	FOUNDING DATE
San Diego de Alcalá	*July 16, 1769*
San Carlos Borromeo de Carmelo	*June 3, 1770*
San Antonio de Padua	*July 14, 1771*
San Gabriel Arcángel	*September 8, 1771*
San Luis Obispo de Tolosa	*September 1, 1772*
San Francisco de Asís	*June 29, 1776*
San Juan Capistrano	*November 1, 1776*
Santa Clara de Asís	*January 12, 1777*
San Buenaventura	*March 31, 1782*
Santa Bárbara Virgen y Mártir	*December 4, 1786*
La Purísima Concepción de Maria Santísima	*December 8, 1787*
Santa Cruz	*August 28, 1791*
Nuestra Señora de la Soledad	*October 9, 1791*
San José de Guadalupe	*June 11, 1797*
San Juan Bautista	*June 24, 1797*
San Miguel Arcángel	*July 25, 1797*
San Fernando Rey de España	*September 8, 1797*
San Luis Rey de Francia	*June 13, 1798*
Santa Inés Virgen y Mártir	*September 17, 1804*
San Rafael Arcángel	*December 14, 1817*
San Francisco Solano	*July 4, 1823*

to pueblos or to inland areas. Meanwhile, the missions went into a state of decay, only to be rebuilt years later.

This book will focus on the missions of the Los Angeles area, which includes the present-day communities of San Fernando and Ventura and the city of Los Angeles. A huge port city and California's largest urban center, Los Angeles was once a tiny Spanish pueblo. Today sprawling suburbs, big businesses, and crowded freeways are familiar sights in Los Angeles.

A little more than 200 years ago, Franciscan priests established San Gabriel Arcángel, San Buenaventura, and San Fernando Rey de España in this coastal area. Mission San Gabriel, founded in 1771, became the fourth settlement in the mission chain. San Buenaventura, the ninth mission, got its start in 1782. San Fernando Rey de España was created in 1797 as the seventeenth mission.

Highlights of Present-Day California

- • City
- ⛪ Mission (see list below left)
- ▨ County
- — El Camino Reál
- — U.S. highway

Miles
0 20 40 60 80 100

Kilometers
0 40 80 120

CALIFORNIA MISSIONS

A San Francisco Solano
B San Rafael Arcángel
C San Francisco de Asís
D San José de Guadalupe
E Santa Clara de Asís
F Santa Cruz
G San Juan Bautista
H San Carlos Borromeo
I Soledad
J San Antonio de Padua
K San Miguel Arcángel
L San Luis Obispo
M La Purísima
N Santa Inés
O Santa Bárbara
P San Buenaventura
Q San Fernando Rey
R San Gabriel Arcángel
S San Juan Capistrano
T San Luis Rey de Francia
U San Diego de Alcalá

PART ONE

Early Life along the Coast

FOR THOUSANDS OF YEARS, THE PRESENT-DAY LOS Angeles area was a natural wilderness. Seals and sea lions barked and splashed off the coast. The ocean teemed with sharks, tuna, halibut, shellfish, and sea mammals. Inland stood oak trees, willows, and cottonwoods.

Birds, rabbits, small deer, and antelope roamed the grassy flatlands. Local waterways—now known as the Santa Clara, the Santa Ana, the San Gabriel, and the Los Angeles Rivers—were filled with salmon, trout, and other freshwater fish. Reeds and tule plants lined the banks of nearby marshes.

Huge oaks spread their leaves over dry, grassy areas of what is now Los Angeles. Coyotes (left inset), *seals* (right inset), **and other animals have long made their homes in this coastal region.**

17

The land was also home to Indians, or Native Americans. Their villages, which usually held from 50 to 500 people, covered the shores and inland areas. The Indians of the Los Angeles region belonged to two main groups, now known as the the Chumash and the Tongva.

Many scientists think that ancestors of the Chumash and Tongva peoples arrived in the Los Angeles area thousands of years ago to hunt game. But Native Americans believe that their people have always been here. Their ancient stories explain that the Creator, who made the earth and the animals, long ago shaped people from the land. The Creator, it was told, had placed the world on the shoulders of seven giants whose movements sometimes caused earthquakes. The people named their powerful god Qua-o-ar or Sup.

Because they had been created from the earth, Indians felt connected to all things on the land. They believed that their Creator had given a spirit to every plant, animal, mountain, lake, and river. Caring deeply for the land, the people took from it only what they needed for survival.

Native American Life

Many Chumash villages once covered the shores of what is now Ventura County and spread northward into central California. The Chumash also lived on four islands off the coast—Santa Cruz, Anacapa, Santa Rosa, and San Miguel.

Tongva peoples lived to the south of the Chumash in a large area that today includes Los Angeles, San Fernando, and much of Orange County.

The Native American groups that inhabited the Los Angeles area didn't give themselves tribal names. Instead they often identified one another by the names of their villages. When the Spaniards arrived, however, they assigned Spanish names to the Indians.

Native Americans near Mission San Gabriel, for example, became known as Gabrielinos. Indians who lived by San Buenaventura were often called Ventureños. The people close to Mission San Fernando were renamed Fernandeños. Most descendants of mission Indians reject these Spanish names. Many Indians in and around the Los Angeles area have kept the name Chumash or now prefer to be known as Tongva.

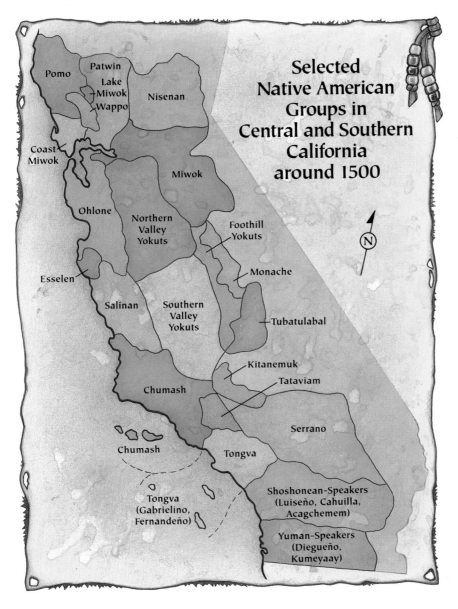

Selected Native American Groups in Central and Southern California around 1500

Pomo
Patwin
Lake Miwok
Wappo
Nisenan
Coast Miwok
Miwok
Ohlone
Northern Valley Yokuts
Foothill Yokuts
Monache
Esselen
Salinan
Southern Valley Yokuts
Tubatulabal
Kitanemuk
Tataviam
Chumash
Serrano
Chumash
Tongva
Tongva (Gabrielino, Fernandeño)
Shoshonean-Speakers (Luiseño, Cahuilla, Acagchemem)
Yuman-Speakers (Diegueño, Kumeyaay)

N

Tongva islanders made their homes on Santa Catalina, San Nicolas, San Clemente, and Santa Barbara Islands.

In these homelands, the Native Americans had all they needed to live. The streams and rivers held a supply of fresh water. Oak trees provided acorns, a main food source. The women gathered elderberries, mushrooms, sage seeds, wild oats, pine nuts, and seaweed for food. The plants were then stored in baskets fashioned from local reeds and grasses.

In the ocean waters swam fish, porpoises, seals, whales, and other sea creatures that the people relied on for food. The forests provided birds and small animals.

Chumash and Tongva hunters used bows and arrows, javelins, curved throwing sticks, clubs, snares, and traps to take game. Feathers and animal skins were made into blankets and clothing.

Because of the warm climate, the Indians wore few clothes. Men wore a simple belt of netting or string from which they hung tools and extra food. Women usually dressed in skirts made from deerskin or the softened bark of cottonwood trees. In cooler months, the people wrapped themselves in capes made from rabbit fur or from the skins of sea otters.

Chumash and Tongva families built their homes from local materials. Bending slender poles fashioned from willows or other trees, the Indians made dome-shaped houses. Builders covered the outside of the dwellings with woven tule. Some houses were large enough to hold as many as 50 people. The homes were cozy, warm, and waterproof.

Chumash and Tongva men built small, earth-covered temescals, or sweat lodges. In these ceremonial buildings, the men sat before a burning fire, which created an intense heat and caused them to sweat heavily.

The Chumash and the Tongva decorated their bodies with red or black paint. Body paint, made from clay and minerals, showed the people's importance or protected their skin from the sun. The Tongva tattooed their foreheads with vertical and horizontal lines. The tattoos were often made by pricking skin with a cactus thorn and rubbing in colored juice squeezed from plant leaves.

Tongva and Chumash Indians found many uses for the yucca plant. The tough leaf fibers, for example, were woven into ropes and baskets.

After their bodies were cleansed, the men jumped into the ocean or a cold stream. This ritual was used before sacred ceremonies or before hunting.

All of the villagers kept clean and healthy by bathing daily. At sunrise people washed in nearby waterways, using the bulb of the amole, or soap plant, to lather up. Villagers dried themselves before a fire while breakfast cooked.

Chiefs ruled the Indian villages. After death, a chief's authority usually passed to his son. If the chief didn't have a son, a daughter or sister could become the leader. Other important villagers included shamans (religious leaders). People relied on the shamans to heal the sick, find food sources, and bring rain. These leaders most often were men, but women could sometimes become shamans, too.

After gathering in the temescal, or sweat lodge, the Indians dove into nearby streams.

The Chumash valued materials such as shells and a soft rock called steatite (soapstone). From shells artisans made a variety of items, including jewelry, ornaments, and money (left). This Chumash bowl (below) was fashioned from steatite.

In the Indian communities, canoe builders and other artisans were held in respect. These craftspeople made artworks, tools, and containers. Women wove baskets of all shapes and sizes, lining them with tar that oozed from local tar pits to make the baskets watertight. Villagers used baskets to carry babies and to store food and water.

Many of the Native Americans carved bowls from the wood of oak trees, made ropes from fibers of the yucca plant, and fashioned small knives from flint. The Chumash placed shells on knife handles and hair ornaments or used the shells as money. Chumash and Tongva villagers created necklaces from abalone, clam, and olivella shells.

Tomols and Ti'ats

To travel to the nearby islands, the mainland Chumash built lightweight canoes known as *tomols*. Constructed from thin planks of pine, tomols were sometimes 30 feet long and were so light that only two people were needed to carry one. Tongva craftspeople also made plank canoes. Their boats were known as *ti'ats*.

The Native American artisans fashioned their canoes without the benefit of iron tools. Using a sharp bone, builders punched holes along the edges of the planks, then lashed the pieces together with plant fibers. By covering the seams with tar, workers made sure the boats were watertight.

From these canoes Chumash and Tongva hunters could spear large fish and sea mammals. The boats also carried goods and people to and from the local islands—to distances of up to 60 miles.

Tomols and ti'ats were lightweight but sturdy.

The Tongva of Santa Catalina Island mined a soft rock called steatite, or soapstone. People used the rock to make bowls, pans, pipes, beads, and carvings. The islanders traded steatite with other groups, including the Chumash.

Tongva families had strong musical traditions. Some of the people crafted flutes, rattles, and other instruments from wood. The Indians sang gambling songs, teaching songs, and lullabies and danced at ceremonies marking special events throughout the year. Their yearly acorn harvest ceremony, for example, was a time for songs, dances, feasts, and reunions with family and friends.

Another important event was the annual mourning ceremony. For eight days, Tongva villagers grieved the loss of the people who had died that year. Women played a special role in the event. Some women, for exam-

The Tongva used materials from the natural world in everyday life. Deer-hoof rattles (top left), for example, were part of religious rituals and celebrations. Chumash shamans (religious leaders) may have painted on rocks (left) in the hills of what is now southern California. These paintings probably held religious meaning.

In daily life, the Chumash villagers worked hard but also found time for rest and games.

ple, sang sacred songs. Others danced and carried bundles of rushes covered with deerskin, which represented the bodies of dead villagers.

The Chumash also held community events. Songs, dances, ceremonies, and games were a major part of Chumash life. Popular games included shinny, played with a hard wooden ball. Another activity was hoop and pole, in which people tried to toss a long pole through a rolling hoop.

The Chumash and Tongva people had strong bonds to their communities, their families, and their homelands. For thousands of years, they thrived and developed time-honored traditions. Elders passed down this heritage from generation to generation.

Newcomers

On September 8, 1771, a small group of Spaniards traveled up the coast of what the Spaniards

Teaching the Children

Chumash and Tongva children didn't go to school or read books to learn the skills needed as adults. Instead children were taught through storytelling and by example. Stories helped young people understand the rewards of proper behavior. Adults set a good example to teach children to be kind, to share freely, and to respect elders.

Each day youngsters learned the skills, crafts, and chores of their village. Older men showed boys how to hunt, fish, and carve hunting tools. Women trained young girls to make baskets and clothing and to gather and prepare food.

Villagers held ceremonies to mark the time when children became young adults. In these rituals, girls were honored with special songs and dances and were taught to be honest and hardworking. The ritual for boys sometimes involved drinking jimsonweed tea, which produced visions. The boys expected their dreams to show them an animal that would become a protector throughout life.

called Alta California. They arrived at a site near the present-day San Gabriel River, a location chosen earlier by Father Junípero Serra, the father-president of the missions. The newcomers had made their way northward from a Franciscan mission located at the San Diego harbor. The group ended up in what is now the Los Angeles area.

The party of Spaniards included two Franciscan missionaries, Father Ángel Somera and Father Pedro Benito Cambón. Ten Spanish soldiers armed with shields and muskets rode on horseback with the priests. Behind them plodded a team of pack mules with four drivers. Four additional soldiers followed, guarding the group from the rear.

Tired and hungry from the long journey up the coast, the Spaniards set up camp. Suddenly the ground began to tremble. Over the next few hours, four separate earthquakes shook the area. The frightened Spaniards called the nearby river Rio de los Temblores, or the River of the Earthquakes. As they tried to remain calm, the men were surrounded by Tongva Indians armed with bows and arrows.

In a defensive move, one of the priests held out a painting of Mary, the mother of Jesus. The Indians immediately set down their weapons, took off the necklaces they wore, and placed their jewelry on the ground before the painting.

The priests believed that this behavior was a sign that the Native Americans would accept the Catholic faith. The priests (or *padres* in Spanish) carried water from the river and blessed the land. They pounded a large cross into the ground. The priests then said mass, marking the founding of San Gabriel Arcángel—the fourth California mission.

When a new mission was established, a priest said mass for the soldiers and Indians.

Many historians have written about the founding of Mission San Gabriel. They reported that the Tongva had placed their necklaces in front of the painting of Mary as a way to worship her and to show their wish to be at peace with the Spaniards. Over the years, many people have accepted this view.

But, as part of their age-old faith, Tongva Indians honored a female spirit called Chukit. Some historians now believe that, when shown the priests' painting, the Indians thought the image was Chukit. They may have intended to honor Chukit by presenting their jewelry as sacred gifts.

PART TWO

Missions of the Los Angeles Area

SAN GABRIEL ARCÁNGEL, SAN BUENAVENTURA, AND San Fernando Rey de España were near the pueblo of Los Angeles, which eventually grew into a bustling city. San Gabriel Arcángel was the earliest of these three missions. It was named for Saint Gabriel, the archangel who is said to have announced the births of both John

A colorful tiled fountain at San Buenaventura stands out against the white-washed adobe walls and the red, tiled roof of the mission.

the Baptist and Jesus. At first Mission San Gabriel suffered from poor crops and from Indian rebellions. But it later prospered and became known as the Pride of the Missions. San Buenaventura, built facing the Pacific Ocean, was named for Saint Bonaventure, an Italian scholar and Franciscan leader who lived in the 1200s. Called the Mission By the Sea, its crops flourished in the region's rich soil and warm climate. San Fernando Rey de España was one of the later settlements in the chain and eventually became one of the largest in Alta California. San Fernando's namesake was Ferdinand III, a thirteenth-century king of Castile (in Spain) who fought against forces occupying his country, built churches, and founded a university.

Mission San Gabriel Arcángel

The Tongva peoples were curious about the Spanish newcomers. Unlike Native Americans, the Spaniards hid their bodies beneath thick layers of clothing. And the soldiers rode horses—animals the Indians had never seen before.

To try to gain the Indians' trust, the Franciscans offered small gifts of beads and clothing. In return Tongva builders helped the missionaries and soldiers construct thatched huts and a temporary chapel. The Spaniards called the Native Americans Gabrielinos, after the mission.

Soon after the founding of Mission San Gabriel, a Spanish soldier attacked the wife of a chief in a Tongva village. Seeking revenge, the chief and other villagers tried to kill the soldier. But the weapons of the Native Americans were no match for the Spaniards'

Each mission used its own hierro, or branding iron. The brand of San Gabriel Arcángel had the letter S curved around the neck of the letter T.

guns. Spanish soldiers shot the chief, cutting off the slain leader's head and placing it on a pole as a warning to others.

A few days later, several Tongva villagers asked the Spanish soldiers for the head of their chief so a mourning ceremony could take place. Afterward the Indians avoided the soldiers and the mission.

Concerned about further conflict, the governor of New Spain sent additional soldiers to San Gabriel Arcángel. But many of the Spanish soldiers lacked discipline and held little respect for Indians. The soldiers rode through Tongva communities and attacked the villagers. Although the Franciscans often complained to government officials about this problem, not much was done to keep the soldiers in line.

At San Gabriel Arcángel, both Father Somera and Father Cambón became ill soon after the founding of the mission and

eventually had to be replaced. The new Franciscans—Father Antonio Cruzado and Father Antonio Paterna—tried to gain the Native Americans' trust through gifts. But, by this time, many Tongva villagers feared

the Spaniards or had little interest in joining the mission.

European diseases began to spread to the Indian villages. The local Native Americans, who had never before been exposed to smallpox and other types of

Highlights of the Los Angeles Area, early 1800s

sicknesses, had no natural resistance to the illnesses. Many Tongva, especially children, became sick and died.

The priests, believing they needed to save the souls of the Indian children, went to the villages and baptized babies. This ritual, in which water is poured over the head, welcomed the person into the religious community. Baptized youngsters who survived their illness then were forced to live at the mission. Parents of newly baptized children began to join San Gabriel Arcángel as a way to keep their families together.

An illustration from the 1800s shows priests baptizing an Indian baby to bring the child into the Roman Catholic community.

Mission Life

The neophytes at Mission San Gabriel helped build a church, a barracks for the soldiers, a granary for storing grain, and living quarters for the priests. The original structures, made from poles and brush, were placed in a four-sided **quadrangle** design. In the center of the quadrangle were 10 huts where mission Indians lived.

The priests taught the neophytes how to farm according to European methods. To clear farmland, the Indians cut down trees and moved large rocks. The neophytes later planted wheat, corn, and vegetables. Workers also dug channels to reroute water from nearby streams to nourish the mission's fields.

Mission San Gabriel's first crops were destroyed by floods. Because supply ships from New Spain were delayed, the mission lacked provisions. Desperate for food, the padres sent the neo-

phytes to gather acorns and pine nuts outside of the mission grounds.

Hoping to escape further flooding, the Franciscans moved the mission five miles away in 1775. The new site in the fertile San Gabriel Valley improved the quality of the mission crops. Neophytes harvested wheat and corn and later produced grapes, olives, and other fruits. The workers also tended growing herds of sheep, goats, and cattle and tanned cattle hides.

Even the neophyte children worked. Young girls, for example, learned to make soap and candles from tallow, or animal fat. Boys helped to look after the fields and to prevent livestock from eating crops.

At San Gabriel Arcángel, neophyte women were responsible for

This sketch shows mission Indians twisting horse hair into ropes. While at the missions, Indian women continued to weave ropes and baskets and to make other crafts. Women also washed clothes and worked in the kitchens.

feeding the entire mission community. They prepared beef and other meat and ground wheat and corn to make a thin, flat bread called a *tortilla*. The women fixed breakfast and dinner in the mission kitchen. Lunch was prepared outdoors in huge kettles. The cooks stirred beef and corn to make a stew called *pozole* and served it with tortillas.

Many of the women and girls had a hard time adjusting to life at Mission San Gabriel. The padres separated six-year-old girls from their families to live in the *monjerio,* or the dormitory where unmarried women stayed. These quarters were hot and crowded.

At the monjerio, a Spanish woman (usually the wife of a soldier) watched over the girls and taught them to spin yarn, sew, and weave. Only after finishing their daily chores could students briefly leave the monjerio to walk around the mission.

The women and girls ate and slept in the monjerio. Every night they were locked in until morning. The secured doors prevented women from escaping and kept men out. In the monjerio, the women and girls weren't allowed to bathe very often. Illnesses quickly spread in the filthy quarters. As a result, the death rate for females at San Gabriel Arcángel was extremely high.

The only way for a neophyte girl to leave the monjerio was to get married. Many girls asked the padres for permission to marry at the age of 15. Married neophyte couples lived outside the mission walls in separate communities. But if a married woman's husband died, she had to return to the monjerio.

(Top left) **A view of the kitchen at San Gabriel Arcángel shows some of the mission's dishware.** *(Bottom left)* **Women cooked food and prepared soap and candles in large kettles.**

Keeper of the Keys

The monjerio at San Gabriel Arcángel was run by the *llavera,* a Spanish word meaning "keeper of the keys." Eulalia Pérez, originally from New Spain, served as the llavera at Mission San Gabriel for 14 years.

Entrusted to hold the monjerio keys, Pérez took care of the girls and made sure they were in the building every night. She also managed the production of food, soap, and clothing for the mission.

One young neophyte, Bartolomea, entered the monjerio at about age six. Although Pérez took a special interest in the girl, Bartolomea had trouble adjusting to life in the monjerio. She left the dormitory at 13, when she married. But for the rest of her life, Bartolomea feared enclosed places because they reminded her of the monjerio.

Eulalia Pérez

35

This way of life was very different from life in Tongva villages, where women bathed daily and gathered food for themselves and their families. Tongva women also had the chance to participate in ceremonies and could sometimes rise to be chiefs or shamans.

Many other neophytes found mission life difficult, too. Each day the ringing of the mission bells told the neophytes when to eat, rest, and work. In the Indian villages, daily life had focused on seasonal routines. Many neophytes missed their old homes and longed to take part in traditional celebrations and dances, which were forbidden at the mission.

The Mission Grows

In 1779 Father Cruzado began constructing a bigger mission church. The new church, designed to look like a Spanish cathedral, was built of stone. It

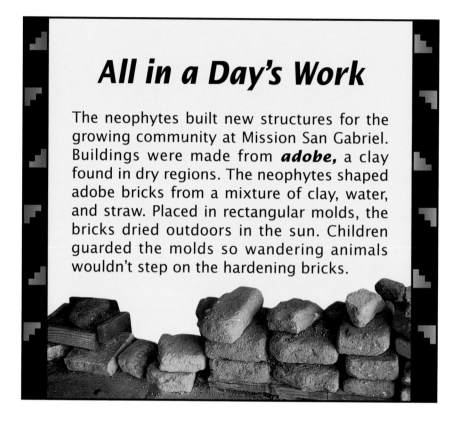

All in a Day's Work

The neophytes built new structures for the growing community at Mission San Gabriel. Buildings were made from *adobe,* a clay found in dry regions. The neophytes shaped adobe bricks from a mixture of clay, water, and straw. Placed in rectangular molds, the bricks dried outdoors in the sun. Children guarded the molds so wandering animals wouldn't step on the hardening bricks.

had long, narrow windows and capped buttresses, or decorative supports, that helped strengthen the walls.

As part of mission life, the neophytes had to attend religious services. During the services, priests performed Catholic ceremonies that included singing and chanting in the Latin language. Although the Indians didn't understand the words, many enjoyed the music that went with Catholic rituals.

The priests also taught the Indians prayers in Spanish. Many neophytes recited the prayers without understanding what the Spanish words meant. In time, however, some Indians learned the Spanish language and acted as translators.

The striking design of the campa-nario (bell wall) at San Gabriel Arc-ángel inspired the building of similar structures at later missions.

The Franciscan priests thought they were doing the Indians a valuable service by teaching them to become Catholic. In fact, the padres believed that this was the greatest gift they could bring to the Native American community.

Because of these beliefs, the padres punished Indians who refused to work hard and to learn Spanish ways. The punishment angered many neophytes, and they sometimes tried to escape. But soldiers brought back the runaways and beat them.

Trouble at the Mission

The neophytes who fled the mission often went back to their old villages and told their people about the hardships at San Gabriel Arcángel. Many Tongva villagers were already angry about the mission because its fields and pastures took up land that Indians had once used for hunting and gathering food.

In 1781 a group of 44 settlers from New Spain arrived in Alta California to start a pueblo near Mission San Gabriel. The government had given the settlers free land and supplies, under the condition that the group would become a self-supporting community.

The site for the new town was known as El Pueblo de Nuestra Señora la Reina de Los Angeles del Río de Porciúncula, or The Town of Our Lady the Queen of the Angels by the River of Porciúncula. Before the Spaniards had arrived, the site had been a Tongva village known by the name of Yang-na.

Reports of suffering at the mission increased the Indians' anger.

In 1785 a neophyte named Nicholas José plotted to overthrow the priests at the mission. He was secretly assisted by a female shaman, Toypurina, who lived in a nearby Tongva village. José organized the neophytes, while Toypurina gathered people from Tongva communities. They planned to attack the mission.

But the Spanish soldiers heard about the raid and captured the Indians. Among the prisoners was Toypurina. Put on trial for her role in planning the revolt, Toypurina expressed the anger that many Tongva felt toward the priests and the mission. Toypurina said, "I hate the padres and all of you, for living here on my native soil, [and] for trespassing upon the land of my forefathers . . . . "

Both Toypurina and José were found guilty of staging the attack. José was condemned to six years of hard labor and, for the rest of his life, was forbidden to see his family. Toypurina went to jail and wasn't let out until she agreed to follow the Cath-

ABOUT THE PRIESTS TOYPURINA—A YOUNG FEMALE SHAMAN—SAID, "I HATE THE PADRES AND ALL OF YOU, FOR LIVING HERE ON MY NATIVE SOIL, FOR TRESPASSING UPON THE LAND OF MY FOREFATHERS, AND DESPOILING OUR TRIBAL DOMAINS."

olic religion and Spanish ways. She took the name Regina Josepha and eventually married a Spanish soldier.

The failed attack didn't change life at the mission. In 1804 workers finished the church. Father Cruzado, who had designed the building and had overseen its progress, died a year before the structure was completed.

Father José María Zalvidea arrived at the mission in 1806 and ran it for the next 20 years. A strict leader, he wanted to continue the mission's agricultural success.

Under his long-term direction, the neophytes ran a large winery, produced a steady supply of soap and candles, and managed huge herds of livestock. Because the mission's cows, sheep, and hogs needed vast amounts of grain for food, San Gabriel Arcángel eventually became the largest producer of grain in Alta California.

The mission thrived, in part, because Father Zalvidea was very demanding of the neophytes. He made sure that the Indians prayed and worked hard and obeyed mission rules. To keep order, the priest chose neo-phyte assistants who beat any-one who sat down on the job or who didn't follow Father Zalvidea's instructions.

It took 16 years to build the church at Mission San Gabriel (right). The earthquake of 1812 severely damaged the structure, and the neophytes worked for many more years to re-build it. A grave (above) on the mis-sion grounds honors the last Indian buried at San Gabriel Arcángel.

During Father Zalvidea's rule, many neophytes died of diseases that the padres, the soldiers, and the Los Angeles settlers carried. Few Indian children survived to adulthood. The hospital built on the mission grounds was often filled with patients.

In 1825 smallpox and cholera swept through the mission, claiming large numbers of neophytes. An estimated three out of every four neophytes at Mission San Gabriel died. Altogether, nearly 6,000 Native Americans were buried at San Gabriel Arcángel.

Mission San Buenaventura

Father Serra had long wanted to establish a mission in Chumash territory, halfway between the missions at San Diego and Monterey. Early reports by Spanish missionaries and soldiers traveling through the region had praised the tomols and crafts of the Chumash.

Father Serra was convinced that the skilled and hardworking Chumash would help a new mission succeed. Delays, however, prevented the founding of San Buenaventura until 1782.

Father Serra traveled the El Camino Reál to the site of the new mission, stopping to rest in Los Angeles and at Mission San Gabriel along the way. With the padre rode 70 soldiers. Families of the soldiers, as well as officials who planned to establish a presidio near the new mission, were also part of the group.

On Easter Sunday, Father Serra raised a large wooden cross in the Chumash settlement of Mitz-kana-kan. He blessed the site and dedicated the mission. The ceremony, which took place on March 31, 1782, marked the founding of the ninth California mission.

Each spring workers rounded up calves at Mission San Buenaventura to brand the animals.

Father Serra appointed Father Cambón, an expert on irrigation methods, to manage the mission. The mission site, chosen because it sat near the coastal villages of the Chumash, wasn't close to a river. Although the mission had a supply of drinking water from local creeks, the settlement's crops needed a larger water source. Father Cambón would have to figure out how to channel water from the Ventura River, located more than five miles away.

Building the Mission

In exchange for gifts of beads or clothing, the Chumash Indians helped the Spaniards build temporary mission structures of poles and thatch. But the Chumash showed little interest in joining the mission. In the first nine months after its founding, the mission recorded only two baptisms.

At the end of the second year, only 22 neophytes were living at San Buenaventura. By 1786 more Chumash had joined the settlement. Nevertheless, 40 percent of the local Chumash population never became part of the mission system.

To find workers, the priests often hired local Chumash. Chumash artisans helped build structures at the Spanish settlement in return for goods. The workers, for example, sometimes performed tasks in exchange for knives, axes, and needles. The Indians found these metal goods useful for daily activities in Chumash communities.

In the early 1790s, construction began on the mission's permanent church, which Chumash workers built using adobe and stone. They cut huge pine trees in forests farther north. Teams of oxen hauled the logs, used for the church's ceiling beams, to the site.

Other structures at the mission included granaries, adobe homes for neophytes, and special quarters for the priests. From the early 1790s until sometime in the early 1800s, the Chumash near San Buenaventura also worked on another major project that would take years to complete—the water system.

Bringing Water to the Mission

The Spaniards at San Buenaventura needed water from local

Mission San Buenaventura wasn't by a river and so had a hard time getting water. Father Cambon's answer was to build a complex water system called an aqueduct. He didn't stay long enough to finish the job, which fell to engineers from New Spain.

streams and rivers for drinking, washing, and irrigating fields. At this mission and others, obtaining water was a major task because local waterways often dried up during the hot summer months. Establishing and storing a water supply required the work of many Indians, who built the dams and ditches.

San Buenaventura relied on the waters of the distant Ventura River and on nearby creeks. Early in the mission's history, Chumash workers dug ditches that led from the Ventura River to San Buenaventura and then built dams of logs and stones to direct the flow of water toward the mission.

In the early 1790s, however, workers began building a more complex water system at San Buenaventura. That year expert engineers and stonemasons from New Spain taught the Indians to strengthen the original brush-and-log dams by adding rocks and limestone cement. Workers

High on a hill behind San Buenaventura loomed a large pine cross, but no one knows for sure when this marker was set up. The Spanish called the hill La Loma de la Cruz, or the Hill of the Cross. Sailors on the Pacific Ocean and travelers on land could see the cross from miles away.

then learned to construct an aqueduct—a system of ditches, clay pipes, and channels for carrying water from the river to the mission.

To form the aqueducts, neophytes lined ditches with rocks, sand, and cement. Workers then put in place long clay pipes through which the water flowed. The neophytes used additional rocks, sand, and cement to secure the pipes in the trench.

The engineers came up with a way to channel the water across the rugged terrain of hills and valleys that lay between the river and the mission. A system of aboveground aqueducts allowed water to flow at a steady pace over areas of high and low land. The aqueducts, which resembled thick walls, were made of boulders and small round stones sealed together with a lightweight cement.

A clay pipe inside the wall allowed the water to flow through the structure. The water traveled slowly by force of gravity.

In order to keep the water moving at the same incline, workers built the aqueduct wall as high as necessary according to the terrain. In valleys the wall sometimes reached as high as 14 feet. On hills and high ground, the wall was much lower. Massive buttresses (supports) on the sides of the wall kept it upright.

The water that arrived at San Buenaventura was stored in reservoirs until needed. One kind of reservoir was a naturally formed pond. Another reservoir at the mission was a shallow pit dug into the ground and lined with stone or plaster. A third kind was made of brick or stone and sat above the ground. Workers sealed the pool-like structure with plaster and cement to make it watertight.

From the reservoirs the water flowed through pipes into a large brick building that contained the settling tank. Before entering the tank, the water passed through a mesh screen that trapped dirt and other debris. Experts believe that the workers may have covered the

Parts of San Buenaventura's water system, including the aqueduct wall (facing page) **and pipes (right), survive.**

bottom of the tank with charcoal and crushed granite to help trap other impurities and further clean the water.

The purified water flowed through a spout out of the building that held the settling tank. Neophyte women collected the clean water to use for drinking and cooking. The reservoir water also flowed to five different fountains and several wash basins at the mission.

At the wash basins, women scrubbed and rinsed clothes in two separate pools. The dirty wash water flowed into another pool, where the dirt and soap settled to the bottom. The clean water was then channeled to the mission's fields through canals. This system was used at other missions as well.

Valves controlled the amount of water released from the canals into a row of grapevines or olive trees. Several hundred acres of cropland at San Buenaventura were irrigated this way.

With plentiful water from the aqueducts, the mission produced many kinds of tropical fruits and vegetables. Bananas,

A VISITOR TO MISSION SAN BUENAVENTURA IN THE 1800S WROTE OF THE ABUNDANCE OF "APPLES, PEARS, PEACHES, POMEGRANATES . . . PRICKLY PEARS, AND GRAPES."

sugarcane, dates, and pomegranates thrived at San Buenaventura. A visitor to the mission in 1793 described the gardens as the finest he had ever seen.

Mission Life

In 1806, while construction of the aqueducts was still taking place, Father José Señán arrived to oversee San Buenaventura. He was generally a well-liked and well-respected Franciscan priest. One father-president wrote that Father Señán was ". . . religious, a good worker, [and] well-fitted to serve as a missionary. . . ." Father Señán led San Buenaventura for 27 years.

During this time, the priest was appointed to serve as father-president of the missions. He held this office for three years, then asked for permission to retire. By 1820 he was again elected as father-president, and he served until his death in 1823.

While at San Buenaventura, Father Señán worked to convert more Chumash to the Catholic faith. At the same time, he allowed the neophytes more freedom than Indians at many other missions were given. He permitted the neophytes to openly practice some of their traditions and to visit their villages often.

The settling tank at San Buenaventura sat in a small brick building with an arched roof. From the tank water flowed out of a stone spout. A Chumash artisan had crafted the water spout in the shape of a horse's head. The building that held the tank became known as El Caballo, meaning "the horse" in Spanish. After San Buenaventura's entire water system had been destroyed by floods in the 1860s, the building was used as a jail. Its prisoners considered El Caballo a hopeless, damp dungeon.

El Caballo (left) still stands, although the horse-head spout is gone. The structure is the oldest building in the present-day city of Ventura. Visitors can also view the restored bell tower (above) of the mission church, which was rebuilt after the 1812 earthquake that damaged structures throughout the Los Angeles area.

(Above) **A sketch made in 1829 shows how San Buenaventura looked at that time, with the mission's towering cross standing on a hill in the background.** *(Inset)* **The Hill of the Cross today.**

Chumash men at the mission continued to build sweat lodges as they had done in their own villages. Many neophyte families at the mission also farmed their own small plots of land. Here they grew favorite crops such as watermelons and sweet potatoes.

For one of the mission fountains, Indian artisans carved a statue of a bear—an animal spiritually important to the Chumash—rather than the usual image of a Catholic saint. And when the last roof tile was placed on the church, Father Señán let the Indians stage a traditional dance in celebration.

Although given some freedom, the Indians were still under the control of the priest. Some of the neophytes tried to escape Spanish rule by running away from the mission. Soldiers caught the runaways and then beat them or put them in jail. Risking punishment, some Chumash neophytes held fast to their traditional religion and beliefs while at the mission.

In December 1812, a major earthquake struck. It caused severe damage to the aqueduct and the buildings at the mission. Father Señán and the neophytes left San Buenaventura and found shelter a few miles inland, where they built a temporary church. During the following year, they repaired the mission buildings and water system.

Other troubles soon occurred. In 1818 Father Señán received word that a pirate named Hippolyte de Bouchard was sailing toward the mission to raid church treasures and mission goods. Before fleeing the mission, the neophytes hid church valuables and filled baskets with food.

Mohave Traders

In the spring of 1819, a group of 21 Mohave Indians arrived at San Buenaventura from their village to the east. They carried blankets and beads to trade with the mission Indians. But mission rules prevented neophytes from interacting with nonmission Indians. The Franciscans feared that outsiders might influence the neophytes to give up Spanish ways and to return home.

As a result, the soldiers at San Buenaventura refused the request and placed the Indians in the guardhouse. The next morning, while most of the soldiers were in church, a guard took a blanket belonging to one of the Mohave prisoners. A fight broke out among the soldiers and Indians, and two soldiers were killed.

Soldiers and neophytes then surrounded the guardhouse. During the conflict, a neophyte named Nicolas Factor was killed, along with 11 Mohave Indians. The remaining Mohave escaped, but four of them were later captured and sent to the presidio at Santa Barbara for punishment.

Father Señán and the neophytes then herded the mission livestock into the hills. After staying away from the mission for a month, the group returned to find that the pirates had left the mission unharmed.

Father Señán's death in 1823 ended his long leadership at San Buenaventura. His fellow priests and many of the neophytes mourned the loss of the respected priest. Father Señán was buried in the mission church near the altar.

Mission San Fernando Rey de España

Vaqueros, *or cowboys, at San Fernando Rey de España marked cattle with this symbol.*

After Father Serra had died in 1784, Father Fermín Francisco de Lasuén became the new father-president of the missions. Father Lasuén was particularly busy during 1797. That year he founded four missions, including San Fernando Rey de España. Established on September 8, 1797, the mission was located about halfway between the missions of San Gabriel and San Buenaventura.

The site for San Fernando Rey de España had actually been chosen 30 years earlier. A group of Spaniards scouting the area had seen that four springs flowed nearby and realized that the water could nourish crops.

Some Tongva in the region now viewed joining a mission as the only way to survive. More than 26 years had passed since the founding of nearby Mission San Gabriel, whose livestock now grazed on land that earlier had supported hunting and gathering. Lacking food, several Tongva families agreed to have their children baptized at the founding of Mission San Fernando.

Neophytes learned to raise livestock and to plow the mission's fields—tasks that weren't part of their traditional way of life. Over time many Indians lost touch with their age-old customs.

Indians continued to come to the mission as a way to get food. In addition, European diseases had caused illness among the Tongva. Because Tongva shamans were unable to cure the sick, some of the people lost faith in their own healers and traditions. Tongva communities suffered greatly, and the villagers went to the mission looking for a way to survive.

Mission Buildings

Father Francisco Dumetz and Father Juan Cortés took charge of San Fernando Rey de España. A large neophyte workforce at the mission quickly constructed buildings. Within just a year, the neophytes had built an adobe church, a storeroom, a weaving room, and a granary. Tile-roofed workshops and barracks for the soldiers soon sat along the mission quadrangle.

The original church became too small to seat the growing

Mission San Fernando's convento, or priests' quarters, hummed with activity. The long building was a favorite stopping place for weary travelers seeking shelter.

number of neophytes at the mission, so workers built a new one in 1800. Within the next few years, about 1,000 neophytes were living at Mission San Fernando.

These Indians constructed an even larger church, which was dedicated in 1806. During the huge celebration that followed, neophyte musicians from nearby missions entertained the large audience with songs and dances.

In 1810 neophytes at San Fernando Rey de España began working on the *convento,* or the building that housed the priests. Conventos usually sat next to the mission church. But at Mission San Fernando, the convento was located on the opposite side of the quadrangle, facing El Camino Reál. Weary travelers often stopped at San Fernando Rey de España's convento to spend the night.

Because the Franciscans kept adding rooms for visitors to the convento, construction on the building took 12 years to complete. Mission San Fernando's convento—which was 243 feet long and 50 feet wide—became known as the "long building." It was probably the largest mission structure ever built.

The two-storied convento had more than 20 rooms, with 14 rooms on the first floor alone. Among them were the priests' bedrooms, a small chapel, a winery, and a kitchen with a huge fireplace for curing and smoking meat. Storerooms and guest rooms were situated on the second floor.

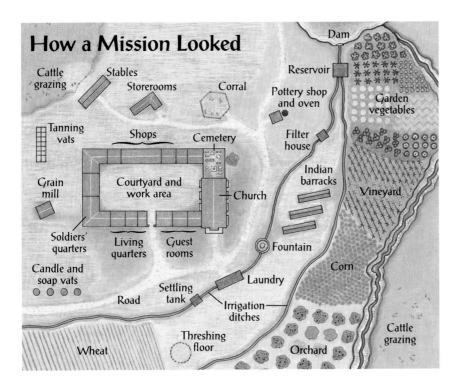

How a Mission Looked

Cattle grazing
Stables
Storerooms
Corral
Dam
Reservoir
Pottery shop and oven
Garden vegetables
Tanning vats
Shops
Cemetery
Filter house
Grain mill
Courtyard and work area
Church
Indian barracks
Vineyard
Soldiers' quarters
Living quarters
Guest rooms
Fountain
Candle and soap vats
Corn
Settling tank
Laundry
Road
Irrigation ditches
Cattle grazing
Wheat
Threshing floor
Orchard

Each of California's 21 missions was slightly different, but they all had common elements. This artwork shows how the mission quadrangle and lands were typically arranged. Priests set aside tracts of land to use for pastures and for fields. Local water supplies were harnessed to provide water for washing, cooking, and irrigation. Workshops sat within and beyond the main mission buildings.

The main entrance of the convento featured giant double doors that opened onto the *sala,* or main room. The sala at Mission San Fernando was the largest reception room of any of the missions. Here the priests greeted visitors with a basin, a pitcher of water for washing, and a glass of wine. Guests at the San Fernando convento stayed for free, so it was always a busy place.

Mission Art

The neophytes, many of whom were talented artisans, created designs on the outside walls of the convento and painted the guest rooms with blue and red patterns. The artists covered several convento walls with designs of vines and flowers.

Paintings of animals, triangles, hunting scenes, or the sun decorated other areas of the building. The neophytes also painted pictures of seashells

above the convento doorways. Wavy lines adorned walls and window arches.

Artists also decorated the mission church. Doorways and window arches were brightly painted. Patterns of checks and diamonds colored red, yellow, white, and blue lined the walls, ceilings, and woodwork.

Although some of these paints came from New Spain, most of them were made by the neophytes themselves. At the missions, the neophytes ground clay and minerals into a fine powder, mixing in water and

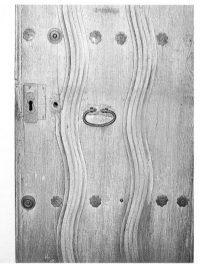

Neophytes painted the walls (top) *of Mission San Fernando. Wavy lines on walls and on doorways* (above) *were a common artistic theme.*

cactus juice. The juice helped the paint mixture stick together.

Many neophyte artists at the various missions decorated the church walls and the other buildings. This artwork was often a combination of European and Native American styles. Murals on church walls, for example, usually showed Christian religious scenes. At Mission San Fernando, however, neophytes also painted a figure of an Indian with a bow near a door in the sala.

One of the most famous examples of neophyte mission art was the work of Juan Antonio, a neophyte at San Fernando Rey de España. He painted the 14 Stations of the Cross—a series of paintings showing the stages that led to the death of Jesus. Antonio's work appeared on

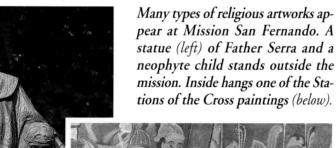

Many types of religious artworks appear at Mission San Fernando. A statue (left) of Father Serra and a neophyte child stands outside the mission. Inside hangs one of the Stations of the Cross paintings (below).

A painting in the Stations of the Cross by Juan Antonio shows Jesus carrying the cross. In the picture, the face of Jesus has Native American features. Some historians believe that the art shows that Antonio had accepted the Catholic faith. Other experts view his work as a way of illustrating that the neophytes, like Jesus, suffered.

canvas sails from a ship anchored in the nearby harbor.

Mission Life

Mission San Fernando was famous for its hides and tallow—products that came from large cattle herds that grazed the mission's lands. The Indians fashioned rawhide strips and tanned the cattle hides to make shoes and saddles. The rawhide was used instead of nails or spikes to hold boards together. All of the

roof beams in the convento, for example, were fastened with this material.

Mission Indians at San Fernando Rey de España also produced cloth, brick, tile, and soap. The mission had 70 acres of olive trees, whose fruits were crushed to make olive oil. Vineyards at the mission produced several kinds of grapes for wine.

Neophytes dumped the ripe grapes into large vats, or tubs. Using their feet, the workers crushed the fruit until the juice

Blacksmiths at Mission San Fernando fashioned iron tools.

dribbled from the bottom of the vat into special wooden troughs.

The workers stored the juice in barrels in a cellar until the liquid had fermented into wine. Mission San Fernando produced both red and white wines. Wine was used for church services, taken as medicine, or traded to other missions.

Mission San Fernando had a large blacksmith shop, where the workers pounded iron into tools, plows, and branding irons. The branding irons, when

Neophyte women wove cloth on the loom at Mission San Fernando.

heated, burned a special mark onto the mission's cattle. In this way, the animals could be identified when lost, stolen, or sold.

San Fernando Rey de España's neophytes became well known for their decorative iron grillwork. The artisans crafted iron bars for mission windows. Some of the bars featured small iron scrolls and flowers that curved outward from the window in graceful patterns. One visitor to the mission remarked that the beautiful decorations looked like they had been crafted in preparation for a *fiesta,* or festival.

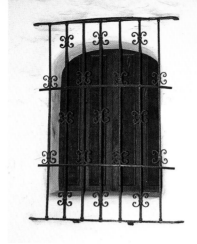

Mission San Fernando was known for its fancy iron grillwork.

Neophyte craftspeople and farmers labored without pay for about eight hours each day at Mission San Fernando. The Indians weren't used to this type of work, however. In their villages,

many tasks—such as hunting and acorn gathering—required effort and energy, but these activities weren't done every day of the year. Many of the neophytes disliked being forced to work so much and had trouble adjusting to their new schedules.

Some neophytes rebelled by refusing to work or by working very slowly to avoid being productive. Neophytes who failed to work hard enough were usually whipped. Those who were punished served as an example to other neophytes who didn't follow the rules.

The Franciscans at San Fernando and the other missions thought that learning the value of hard work would benefit the Indians. The padres believed that one day the missions would be turned over to the neophytes, who would have to know how to farm, raise livestock, and construct buildings. As it turned out, that day came sooner than the priests had planned.

The padres at San Fernando Rey de España had trouble keeping rats out of the granary, where grain was stored. To solve the problem, the priests borrowed some cats from nearby Mission San Gabriel. The padres then cut holes in the bottom corners of the mission doors so the cats could come and go as they pleased. The holes can still be seen at the mission.

PART THREE

Secularization of the Missions

IN THE EARLY 1800S, PEOPLE IN NEW SPAIN WERE struggling for independence from Spain. During the long conflict, government officials in New Spain used most of their money to pay for troops and military equipment.

The government leaders didn't have time to worry about the needs of the missionaries and settlers in Alta California. As a result, New Spain usually ignored the Franciscans' requests for supplies.

But the priests at the missions of San Gabriel, San Fernando, and San Buenaventura wanted provisions such as tools and books.

In the late 1820s, Mission San Gabriel was a self-sufficient community with productive lands and many workers.

The Franciscans began to trade with French, British, and Russian ships on the coast, even though Spanish law forbade it. Through this foreign trade, the missions became self-sufficient.

The presidios and pueblos weren't able to support themselves, however. Instead they came to rely on the the thriving missions for basic provisions. Local residents, known as Californios, depended on the missions to provide food, clothing, and other supplies.

In pueblos such as Los Angeles, for example, the Californios wanted fruits and vegetables, meat, wine, and shoes. The people looked to the missions for these items. The Franciscans, when they could, even paid the salaries of the soldiers who lived in nearby pueblos and presidios.

But having to rely on the missions caused the soldiers and Californios to feel resentful. They looked longingly at the missions' productive fields and healthy herds. The Californios wanted this property to be divided up and given to them.

Secularization Laws

In 1821 New Spain gained its independence from Spain, eventually becoming the Republic of Mexico. As a new nation, Mexico gained control of Alta California.

Mexican officials wanted to strengthen their claim to the region by sending more Mexicans to settle farms and towns in Alta California. Mexico's leaders realized, however, that the region's most fertile farmland was under the control of Franciscan priests.

To gain mission land, the Mexican government planned to pass laws to secularize the missions. These laws would al-

A group of settlers known as Californios relax on a porch at Mission San Fernando in the 1800s.

low the Mexican government—not the Franciscans—to control mission property. The government wanted to give some plots to Mexican settlers, some to the Californios, and some to the neophytes.

With the new laws, the Franciscans would have to turn over their churches to secular, or parish, priests who didn't do missionary work. In addition, the neophytes would be free to leave the missions.

Most of the Franciscan priests argued against secularization. They thought of the neophytes as children who needed supervision. The Franciscans also worried that, if allowed to leave the missions, the Indians might give up the Catholic faith and return to their old ways. The Mexican government planned to secularize the missions anyway.

But at the same time, Mexican officials realized the problems involved in breaking down the mission system. Most neo-phytes had never lived outside mission walls, had never been taught to read, and had never owned their own property. Mexican leaders thought that the neophytes lacked the skills to live and work outside of the

IN THE EARLY 1800S, THE FRANCISCANS FEARED THAT, IF ALLOWED TO LEAVE THE MISSIONS, THE INDIANS MIGHT GIVE UP THE CATHOLIC FAITH AND RETURN TO THEIR OLD WAY OF LIFE.

missions. These officials also feared that the freed Indians might gather with other Native Americans and revolt against non-native people.

By 1823 the neophytes at the 21 missions totaled about 21,000—far outnumbering all the padres, soldiers, and settlers in Alta California. Mexico feared that these Native Americans could overpower the non-native population.

As a result, the government planned to treat the Indians fairly and to provide them with land, livestock, and tools to help them succeed. The Californios grew angry, however, because they wanted the majority of mission farmland and ranchland for themselves.

In 1834 Governor José Figueroa of Alta California announced a plan to immediately secularize 10 missions, with the other 11 to follow soon after. The Mexican government then placed civil administrators in charge at each mission. They were supposed to distribute the farmland and supplies among the ex-neophytes and the local citizens.

But many ex-neophytes didn't want to work as farmers any

longer. Most simply wanted to return to their old villages and live among their people. Some Indians gambled away their property and ended up poor. Others lost their land grants through the trickery of land-hungry Californios.

In addition, many administrators cared more about themselves than about the missions or helping the ex-neophytes. These overseers often took control of land that rightly belonged to the former mission Indians. Left without property, many Native Americans ended up working as servants in the homes of the Californios.

At the Missions

Father Tomás Esténega, the last priest in charge of Mission San Gabriel, turned over the mission's property to the government in 1834. The monjerios at San Gabriel Arcángel closed, and young girls and women were free to live with their families again.

The church at Mission San Gabriel, however, wasn't completely deserted. A few old women, some orphaned children, and some neophytes too sick to leave stayed on and took care of the building.

Much of the mission slowly fell into ruin. When Mexican administrator Juan José Rocha took over in 1834, for example, Mission San Gabriel had 16,500 head of livestock. But eight years later, only 72 cattle and 700 sheep remained.

Much of the livestock and produce had been sold to pay the salaries of the administrators. The once bustling mission workshops were now silent.

San Buenaventura was also secularized in 1834. Some of the neophytes went to work on nearby ranchos as cowhands. Others headed eastward to join large groups of Native Americans who had set up Indian communities farther inland. For the next 26 years, ownership of San Buenaventura passed back and forth between different landowners, although services

A civil administrator, or mission overseer, urges a group of ex-neophytes to get to work.

continued to be held at the mission church.

One administrator at San Buenaventura was Carlos Carrillo. Almost immediately after assuming this position, he was named governor of Alta California and resigned from San Buenaventura. But the former governor—Juan Bautista Alvarado—refused to leave office.

Alvarado and Carrillo prepared for battle, gathering about 100 supporters each. Carrillo's troops barricaded themselves inside San Buenaventura, and Alvarado's men surrounded the mission. Each side fired cannons for two days.

Carrillo's fighters later slipped away from the mission under cover of darkness, ending the battle. Governor Alvarado remained in office for four more years. Carrillo was replaced at Mission San Buenaventura by an administrator named Rafael Gonzales. Gonzales sold most of the mission property to settlers.

In 1834 the Franciscans turned over Mission San Fernando to Antonio Del Valle. Under this administrator, the mission church fell apart. He let settlers steal roof tiles for their own houses. Without the protection the tiles had offered, the adobe walls of the church wore away from rain and wind, and the building slowly collapsed.

Another administrator at San Fernando—Francisco Lopez—discovered gold near the mission in March 1842. As word spread of his find, gold seekers arrived from Los Angeles and other nearby towns. These newcomers further damaged the church by digging for gold beneath its floor.

The Mexican government realized that under the administrators the missions weren't producing the food and supplies still needed by many soldiers and settlers. In 1843 Mexican officials gave 12 of the missions, including San Gabriel Arcángel

Pío Pico, one of the last governors of Mexican California, disliked the mission system.

and San Buenaventura, back to the Franciscans. The government hoped that the priests could increase the production of goods once again.

Franciscan control didn't last long, however. By 1846 Pío Pico—one of the last governors of Mexican California—had sold Missions San Gabriel and San Buenaventura to settlers from the United States. He used some of the money to pay off his own debts and kept the rest for profit. By 1847 Pico had also sold Mission San Fernando.

Meanwhile, Mexico and the United States were at war. During the Mexican War, U.S. naval forces landed on the coast of Alta California to seize control of the region. A peace treaty signed in 1848 officially made Alta California part of the United States.

U.S. Settlement

After the war ended, U.S. settlers poured into Alta California in search of gold. In 1850 the region, now called California, became the thirty-first U.S. state.

Newcomers were soon mining for gold and building farms. In the process, these settlers took control of land that Native American groups had occupied for thousands of years.

With little territory left on which to hunt and gather, the Indians' way of life was threatened. Many traditions that had held Indian communities together in the past were gone,

and Indians were dying from hunger and disease.

Angered by the loss of their people and desperate for food, Native Americans often raided

> *"I WAS DETERMINED TO PUT AN END TO THE MISSION SYSTEM . . . IN ORDER THAT THE LAND COULD BE ACQUIRED BY PRIVATE INDIVIDUALS."*
> GOVERNOR PÍO PICO

ranches and farms for cattle and horses. In response, settlers killed Indians for revenge or simply for sport.

To settle these conflicts, the U.S. government decided to set aside tracts of land for Native Americans. Many of the Indians in California moved to these territories, called **reservations.**

On the reservations, Native Americans often lacked food, medical attention, and basic supplies. By the end of the 1860s, less than 30,000 Indians were left in California. Only several hundred Tongva and Chumash remained, for these groups had nearly died out as a result of poverty, disease, and starvation.

The Missions Decline

U.S. government officials returned Mission San Gabriel to the Roman Catholic Church in 1859. All that remained of the once vast mission was the old church, a few buildings, some workrooms, a garden, and the vineyards. Catholic officials maintained the church but couldn't afford to take care of the other mission buildings. Rooms were rented out to be used as stores or inns.

In 1862 the Catholic Church regained ownership of Mission

San Buenaventura. Although the mission church remained intact, many of the religious artifacts were gone. That same year, the Catholic Church also took control of property that had once belonged to Mission San Fernando Rey de España, including the old mission church, the convento, and the cemetery.

For the next few years, the Catholic Church rented out much of Mission San Fernando's property to the Butterfield Stagecoach line. Travelers going from Los Angeles northward to San Francisco boarded their coaches at the mission.

By the end of the 1800s, the three missions of the Los Angeles area were surrounded by bustling new communities. The once thriving buildings and fields of San Gabriel Arcángel, San Buenaventura, and San Fernando Rey de España had largely crumbled and decayed. But each mission was about to begin a new chapter of its history.

During the Mexican War (1846–1848), John C. Frémont of the U.S. Army used the convento at Mission San Fernando as his headquarters. Other buildings at San Fernando Rey de España fell apart after the war because nearby settlers took tiles and roof beams.

In 1883 four generations of Indian women were living in this dwelling near Mission San Gabriel.

PART FOUR

The Missions in Modern Times

BY THE LATE 1800s, THE PROSPEROUS DAYS OF THE missions and ranchos were long gone. U.S. settlers had taken over California and were successfully farming the land and mining for gold. Ex-neophytes and other Native Americans were suffering from disease and poverty on the reservations.

A writer named Helen Hunt Jackson wanted people to understand how poorly Indians in California had been treated. To show readers the hardships the Indians were facing, she published *Ramona,* a story set in early California.

In one of his many paintings of the California missions, artist Edwin Deakin portrayed San Fernando Rey de España in ruins. The haunting beauty of his artworks helped fuel public interest in the missions.

The book was so popular that readers became enthusiastic about California's mission past. Instead of caring about the Indians, however, people simply wanted to see the old Spanish missions. Many of these tourists stole adobe bricks or roof tiles to take home. The old buildings began to crumble even further.

In the Los Angeles region, the churches at San Gabriel Arcángel and San Buenaventura had remained in use and so were in better shape than most other mission churches. Nevertheless, an official from the Los Angeles Public Library wanted to reconstruct these historic buildings and in 1893 asked publisher Charles F. Lummis for help. Lummis launched the Landmarks Club, which worked to preserve the missions and other old structures of California.

During that same year, Father Ciprian Rubio of Mission San Buenaventura decided to make

The Missions in Words and Art

Helen Hunt Jackson visited the California missions and many nearby ranches in the 1880s. She talked to former neophytes and to other Indians, who were losing their land to U.S. settlers. Indian land, in her opinion, had been unfairly taken away. Also concerned about conditions on the reservations, Jackson wanted the Indians to receive more land, more education, and better farm tools. She presented her views to U.S. lawmakers.

When her message failed to change government policies toward Indians, Jackson tried another way. In 1884 she published her famous love story, *Ramona*, to show through fiction the hardships Indians faced. The novel became a bestseller. It brought

tourists from all over the nation and inspired Californians to capture the story on postcards and in plays.

Meanwhile, Edwin Deakin, a famous English painter, had moved to the United States, eventually ending up in San Francisco. There he became fascinated by the ruins of the nearby California missions. By about 1900, he had painted each of the 21 missions.

Deakin's style of painting evoked a mysterious and tender mood. By showing the missions in ruins, he inspired a longing to see the old buildings. Magazine stories about Deakin's work increased the public's desire to visit the mission ruins.

Author Helen Hunt Jackson (facing page) *wrote the best-seller* Ramona. *Edwin Deakin painted San Buenaventura* (left) *and the other 20 missions.*

his church more modern. First the priest added larger windows to let in more light. Then he covered the floor and the ceiling with wood paneling. Father Rubio also tore out the church's original handcarved wooden pulpit and painted over the Native American designs on the mission walls.

Meanwhile, the excitement to revive the missions spread. By the early 1900s, people near San Buenaventura had mounted a new cross on the Hill of the Cross. Cut from Jeffrey pines, the 26-foot cross was designed to last about 100 years.

This photo from the late 1800s shows the quadrangle of San Buenaventura before it was modernized.

By the 1890s, little was left of the church at Mission San Fernando. The roof timbers had collapsed. People had removed the roof tiles to use elsewhere and had dug up the floor in search of treasure.

At San Gabriel Arcángel, priests of the Claretian religious order took over the mission in 1908. Under the leadership of Father Raymond Catalan, the priests unearthed many parts of the original buildings. Buried underneath piles of rubble and adobe mud were foundation walls, tile floors, and the remains of Mission San Gabriel's old water system.

By 1916 the Landmarks Club was raising money to save Mission San Fernando's crumbling church. A special event was planned in which 6,000 people each bought a candle and marched through the ruins of Mission San Fernando after dark to show their commitment to restoring the building. The money earned from the candles helped pay for the restoration.

At San Fernando Rey de España, an experienced adobe builder made thousands of adobe bricks to repair the crumbling walls of the church. Another worker chipped away layers of whitewash and plaster to uncover original murals painted by the neophytes. Other workers laid tiles on the church floor and rebuilt the mission's campanario.

Most mission restorers simply wanted to make the missions attractive to the public. The workers didn't always follow historical accounts to reconstruct the buildings. As a result, the restored missions are a blend of history and imagination.

The Missions Now

The church of San Gabriel Arcángel now sits in the city of San Gabriel. Some of the regular worshipers are descendants of mission Indians, who hold a fiesta at the church every year.

They also pay respect to their ancestors at the mission cemetery—the oldest cemetery in Los Angeles County—where nearly 6,000 Indians are buried. Many of their descendants are disappointed that the Roman Catholic Church hasn't placed a marker over the mass graves of the mission Indians who long ago died of sickness here.

Inside the church at San Gabriel stands the original pulpit from which the first padres preached to the neophytes. The altar holds six religious statues brought from Spain in 1791. On the walls hang 300-year-old paintings from Spain. Other decorations include an old copper baptismal font, or basin, which was a gift from the Spanish king Charles III in 1771.

Visitors to the mission of San Gabriel can view the original

winery and the open fireplace where cooks prepared the noon meal. The tannery still exists, along with parts of the original aqueduct. But four deep holes lined with brick are all that remain of the mission's soap and tallow factory. Neophytes once built fires in the holes to heat kettles full of tallow.

Three grape arbors shade the garden pathways at the mission. These vines came from the original plants sown at the site. Mission San Gabriel also features a patio filled with tropical plants and cacti. Although the original mission probably didn't have such lavish gardens, they help beautify the landscape.

Mission San Gabriel is still affected by earthquakes. In 1987 an earthquake struck the church, closing it for about five years. The mission reopened in 1993 but was hit by a larger earthquake in 1994. The tremors damaged the campanario, the convento, and the church walls.

(Facing page) **Mission San Gabriel became known as the "Pride of the Missions" for its prosperity. Nowadays it's still under repairs for damage caused by recent earthquakes** *(left).* **Visitors can view a statue of Father Junípero Serra** *(below)* **on the mission grounds.**

Earthquakes have also damaged San Fernando Rey de España, located in the city of San Fernando. In 1971 tremors destroyed the church. A hand-carved wooden statue of Saint Ferdinand fell from the altar, and parts of the old artwork cracked.

An expert restorer sifted through the rubble to find 27 pieces of the statue, which he then glued back together. Community members and local businesses donated money to restore the church. By 1974 an exact replica of the original church was standing at the site.

The 1994 earthquake damaged Mission San Fernando's convento and museum. Large cracks appeared on the convento walls, and chunks of plaster fell off in places where the adobe bricks had buckled.

San Buenaventura, in the city of Ventura (formally known as San Buenaventura), still faces

Earthquake damage at Mission San Fernando

Wooden bell at San Buenaventura

the ocean. But the Mission By the Sea no longer has Father Rubio's wood paneling or modern windows. Restorers, guided by Father Aubrey J. O'Reilly, stripped away the paneling to find the original beams and tiles. The builders also reconstructed the windows.

A mission restorer named Harry Downie provided San Buenaventura's church with wooden chandeliers and also designed new doors for the building. On the walls of the church hang Stations of the Cross paintings. Restorer Franz Trevors uncovered the beautiful colors of the 200-year-old artworks that lay beneath age-old layers of mildew, candle smoke, and grime.

Mission San Buenaventura's museum holds two old wooden bells carved from two-foot-thick blocks, but no one knows for sure where the bells came from. Outside the museum looms the

Every year school groups (right) tour the missions of California. Visitors learn about the contributions that the Franciscans made to California history and about the many Indians who lived and died at the missions.

mission's towering cross, which is now surrounded by landscaping and lights. About four miles from the mission are some remains of the old aqueduct walls.

Archaeologists and historians continue to study the missions of San Gabriel Arcángel, San Buenaventura, and San Fernando Rey de España to learn more about their history. Many tourists, students, and churchgoers visit the sites regularly.

These visitors can see for themselves that the missions were the original source of the many vineyards and olive groves throughout the state of California. The missions also inspired the architecture of many buildings in the Los Angeles area and in other parts of California.

The California missions, however, also inspire heated debate. Many Native Americans view them not as monuments but as places that caused death and suffering for thousands of Indians. Although the missions have changed dramatically over the years, each one serves as an important link to California's complex past.

AFTERWORD

Each year thousands of tourists and students visit the California missions. Many of these visitors look around and conclude that the missions are the same today as they were long ago. But, over time, the missions have gone through many changes. The earliest structures were replaced by sturdier buildings with tall towers and long arcades. But even these solid buildings eventually fell into ruin and later were reconstructed.

Our understanding of the missions also has changed through the years. Missionaries, visitors, novelists, and scholars have expressed different opinions about the California missions. These observers often have disagreed about the impact of the missions on the Indians in California. And the voices of Native Americans—from the past *and* the present—have continued to shed light on the mission experience.

The early Franciscan missionaries believed that they were improving the local Indians by introducing them to mission life. But visitors from Europe and the United States frequently described the Spanish missions as cruel places. A French explorer in 1786, for example, reported that the priests treated the neophytes like slaves. He was horrified that Spanish soldiers tracked down runaway Indians and whipped them for trying to return to their old way of life.

Many early visitors were truly concerned about the mistreatment of Native Americans. But the foreign travelers, jealous of Spain's hold on Alta California, also criticized the missions as a way to prove that Spain wasn't worthy to possess the region. Similarly, a young man from the eastern United States, visiting Alta California in the 1830s, was saddened to see so much sickness and death at the missions. He advised his fellow Americans that the region would fare much better as a part of the United States.

The missions were all but forgotten during the 25 years following the U.S. takeover of California. The once solid structures decayed into piles of rotting adobe. One U.S. visitor wrote that she doubted if any structure on earth was "colder, barer, uglier, [or] dirtier" than a California mission.

Just when the missions had disappeared almost completely, they came roaring back to public attention. Beginning in the 1880s, dozens of novels and plays about early California described the Franciscan priests as kind-hearted souls who treated neophytes with gentleness and care. This favorable image of the missions became popular because it gave many Californians a positive sense of their own history and identity. The writings also attracted droves of tourists to California. Merchants and business leaders in the state supported the rebuilding of the crumbling missions because it made good business sense.

The missions today are still the subject of a lively debate. Some people continue to believe that the missions brought many benefits to the Indians by "uplifting" them to European ways. But many others, including some descendants of the neophytes, say that the missions destroyed Native American lifeways and killed thousands of Indians. For all of us, the missions continue to stand as reminders of a difficult and painful time in California history.

Dr. James J. Rawls
Diablo Valley College

CHRONOLOGY

Important Dates in the History of the Missions of the Los Angeles Area

1769   San Diego de Alcalá, the first Franciscan mission in Alta California, is founded by Father Junípero Serra

1771   San Gabriel Arcángel is established

1781   Newcomers set up the pueblo of Los Angeles

1782   Mission San Buenaventura is founded

1784   Father Junípero Serra dies; Father Fermín Francisco de Lasuén becomes the new father-president

1785   Indians near Mission San Gabriel revolt

1797   Father Lasuén founds four new missions, including San Fernando Rey de España

1810   Revolution begins in New Spain

1812   Earthquake hits the Los Angeles area

1821   New Spain gains independence from Spain

1830s   Missions are secularized

1846   Mexican War begins; U.S. Navy occupies Monterey

1848   Mexican War ends; Mexico cedes Alta California to the United States

1850   California becomes the thirty-first state

1850s   U.S. government begins to return the California missions to the Catholic Church; mission buildings are falling apart

1890s–present   Missions are restored

ACKNOWLEDGMENTS

Photos, maps, and artworks are used courtesy of: Laura Westlund, pp. 1, 15, 19, 30, 31, 40, 48, 51; © John Elk III, pp. 2, 53 (left); Southwest Museum, Los Angeles, CA, pp. 8-9 (photo by Don Meyer, CT.374-646.G136), 22 (right) (photo by Lawrence Reynolds, 10.C.53), 24 (bottom); North Wind Picture Archives, pp. 10, 27, 33; Independent Picture Service, pp. 12, 13, 32, 49, 60, 74-75 (photo by Nancy Smedstad); © Eda Rogers, pp. 16-17 (all), 34 (bottom), 36, 45 (left), 46 (bottom), 50, 52 (bottom), 54 (both); 55, 72 (left and right), 73 (both); © Don Eastman, p. 20; Bancroft Library, pp. 21, 46 (top), 63 (left); Santa Barbara Museum of Natural History, p. 22 (left); © Carol Stiver, pp. 23, 34 (top); San Diego Museum of Man, p. 24 (top); Santa Barbara Historical Society, p. 25; © Shirley Jordan, pp. 28, 39 (right), 71 (bottom); Huntington Library, pp. 35, 58, 61; © Chuck Place, pp. 37, 70; © Diane C. Lyell, pp. 39 (left), 72 (middle); Ventura County Museum of History & Art, p. 42; © Charles Fredeen, pp. 43, 52 (top), 71 (top); © Frank L. Lambrecht, p. 45 (right); California Historical Society, Title Insurance and Trust Photo Collection, Dept. of Special Collections, USC Library, pp. 53, 68; Mission Santa Barbara Archives, p. 57; Special Collections, Tutt Library, Colorado College, Colorado Springs, CO, p. 63 (right); Seaver Center for Western History Research, Natural History Museum of Los Angeles County, pp. 65, 67, 69; Library of Congress, p. 66; Diane MacMillan, p. 78 (top); Dr. James J. Rawls, p. 78 (middle); Professor Edward D. Castillo, p. 78 (bottom). Cover: (Front) © Don Eastman; (Back) Laura Westlund.

Quotations are from the original or translated writings of Toypurina, p. 38; Captain George Vancouver, p. 44; Father Estéban Tápis, p. 44; Governor Pío Pico, p. 62.

METRIC CONVERSION CHART		
WHEN YOU KNOW	**MULTIPLY BY**	**TO FIND**
inches	2.54	centimeters
feet	0.3048	meters
miles	1.609	kilometers
square feet	0.0929	square meters
acres	0.4047	hectares
ounces	28.3495	grams
pounds	0.454	kilograms
gallons	3.7854	liters

ABOUT THE AUTHOR

Dianne MacMillan, a former elementary-school teacher, is an accomplished author who has published both fiction and nonfiction children's books. She also pens articles for juvenile magazines and regularly visits classrooms to talk with children about her writing experiences. MacMillan has three daughters and lives with her husband in Orange Park Acres, California.

ABOUT THE CONSULTANTS

James J. Rawls is one of the most widely published and respected historians in the field of California history. Since 1975 he has been teaching California history at Diablo Valley College. Among his publications are *Indians of California: the Changing Image, New Directions in California History,* and, with Walton Bean, *California: An Interpretive History.* Dr. Rawls is also the author of several works for young readers, including *Never Turn Back: Father Serra's Mission* and *California Dreaming.* Dr. Rawls frequently serves as a consultant for books, for television and radio programs, and for film documentaries on subjects dealing with California's history.

Edward D. Castillo is a direct descendant of Cahuilla-Luiseño Indians who lived at Missions San Gabriel and San Luis Rey. A professor of California Indian ethnohistory for more than 20 years, Castillo offers Native perspectives of mission life to students of California history. His first book is entitled *Native American Perspectives on the Hispanic Colonization of Alta California.* He recently cowrote, with historian Robert Jackson, *Indians, Franciscans and Spanish Colonization: The Impact of the Mission System on California Indians.* Professor Castillo is a founding member of the Native American Studies Departments at the Los Angeles and Berkeley campuses of the University of California. At Sonoma State University, he serves as an associate professor and chairs its Native American Studies Department.

INDEX